BOOK ANALYSIS

By Cassandra Gibbons

The Casual Vacancy

BY J.K. ROWLING

Bright
≡Summaries.com

J.K. ROWLING

ENGLISH WRITER

- **Born in Gloucestershire in 1965.**
- **Notable works:**
  - *Harry Potter and the Philosopher's Stone* (1997), fantasy novel
  - *Harry Potter and the Goblet of Fire* (2000), fantasy novel
  - *Harry Potter and the Deathly Hallows* (2007), fantasy novel

J.K. Rowling is an English writer famous the world over for her *Harry Potter* book series. She was born in Gloucestershire in 1965 and wrote stories as a child before studying French and Classics at Exeter University. Her earlier career took her to Portugal, where she taught English as a foreign language, but she returned to the UK when her marriage to a Portuguese journalist failed. Struggling to make ends meet for herself and her daughter, she began writing what would become the *Harry Potter* series in cafés. By the turn of the century she was a hugely successful children's author.

The Casual Vacancy, published in 2012, is Rowling's first novel for adults. She has written four crime novels to date centring on private detective Cormoran Strike. She used the nom de plume Robert Galbraith so as to hide her authorship of the novels, to see if they could be successful without her famous identity attached to them. When she was revealed as the true author, sales naturally skyrocketed. Rowling also has a career in film, working as a producer on the last few films in the *Harry Potter* franchise and turning her hand to screenwriting for the *Fantastic Beasts* film franchise, an expansion of her *Harry Potter* universe.

THE CASUAL VACANCY

A TRAGICOMIC NOVEL

- **Genre:** novel
- **Reference edition:** Rowling, J.K. (2012) *The Casual Vacancy*. London: Little, Brown.
- **1st edition:** 2012
- **Themes:** social breakdown, village life, drug abuse, domestic abuse, sexual abuse, class, local politics

Given that *The Casual Vacancy* was written by one of the richest and most famous authors who has ever lived, it was a highly anticipated publication. Reviews of the novel were mixed, but one million copies were sold in English within a month of publication. In 2015 the novel was adapted into a three-part television series broadcast on the BBC.

The novel is set in Pagford, a small parish council in the South West. The events of the novel are triggered by the death of Barry Fairbrother, a parish councillor who was born in the nearby council estate 'the Fields' and climbed the social ladder to live comfortably in middle-class Pagford with his family. Barry touched the lives of many people around him, and he is the thread that holds the novel together. His parish council seat – the 'casual vacancy' of the title – is bitterly contested between two rival factions: one that wishes to continue Barry's legacy and one that seeks to destroy it.

SUMMARY

THE DEATH OF BARRY FAIRBROTHER

The novel begins with the death of Barry Fairbrother, a local councillor, who collapses in a restaurant car park accompanied by his wife Mary. As the news of Barry's fatal aneurysm spreads, his connections to almost everyone in the town are conveyed in the reactions of various characters. Many people are devastated, like Colin Wall, who, despite his social awkwardness, managed to forge a friendship with Barry. Parminder Jawanda, a GP and fellow councillor, is shocked at how painful she is finding the death of a friend. Krystal Weedon, meanwhile, tries to act like she does not care but is clearly deeply affected by the death of her rowing instructor-cum-mentor. Howard Mollison, on the other hand, is secretly thrilled at Barry's death given that they were political opponents on the council.

A subsection of the first part of the novel entitled 'Olden Days' lays out the central political schism that divides the community. The Fields is an impoverished council estate located between Pagford and Yarvil that belongs, for now, to the parish of Pagford. Barry Fairbrother was born in the Fields and worked his way up the social ladder to reside comfortably in Pagford. He is in favour of keeping the Fields a part of Pagford so that the estate's residents can benefit from St Thomas's, an excellent primary school in Pagford. Howard Mollison wants the Fields reassigned to Yarvil, the nearby town, as he does not want Pagford to have to deal with the social problems of the Fields. He is buoyed in his opinion by the fact that another pupil at St Thomas's who came from the Fields, Krystal Weedon, punched his granddaughter Lexie so hard in the face when they were younger that she lost two teeth. The council was evenly divided on this issue before Barry's death, but Howard now sees an opportunity to tip the balance in his favour.

Meanwhile, three contenders for Barry's empty seat emerge: Colin 'Cubby' Wall, who wants to continue his friend's legacy; Simon Price, who mistakenly believes that being a councillor will pay handsomely in bribes; and Miles Mollison,

Howard's son. All three candidates lack the support of some of their family members. Tessa Wall thinks her husband is not stable enough, nor as charismatic as Barry, to fulfil the role. Colin's adopted son Stuart (also known as Fats) despises his father and would not support him in any endeavour. Simon Price is abusive to his family, and his son Andrew (Fats' best friend) detests his father and predicts that his election attempt will lead to family humiliation. Simon's wife Ruth is encouraging, but only out of fear of her husband's fist. Miles Mollison enjoys the devoted support of his parents Howard and Shirley, but enrages his frustrated wife Samantha, who loathes watching her boring husband slowly morph into her repulsive father-in-law.

The political division in the community is joined by myriad divisions between individual Pagfordians. Shirley Mollison battles with her husband's business partner Maureen for influence over Howard. Fats Wall truants in order to enrage his father and also ruthlessly bullies Sukhvinder Jawanda, Parminder's daughter. Krystal struggles to make her heroin-addicted mother, Terri, see that if she relapses her younger brother Robbie will be taken into care. Newcomer Kay Bawden, who has moved to Pagford from London for a relationship, tries to make her relationship with the unwilling Gavin work while dealing with her daughter's rage at being moved against her will. Even Mary Fairbrother is resentful of her late husband for neglecting his family in favour of helping Krystal Weedon and championing the Fields. These individual family battles and the wider political schism play out at Barry's funeral.

THE GHOST OF BARRY FAIRBROTHER

Despite Howard's hopes to simply install his son Miles in Barry's empty seat, an election is called and the campaigns begin. Barry's last project – a local newspaper interview with Krystal – limps on ahead, but Krystal finds it hard to explain the benefits of keeping the Fields in Pagford without her mentor there to guide her. Kay, who is the Weedons' social worker, goes for dinner at the Mollisons' and is outraged that they are in favour not only of reassigning the Fields to Yarvil, but also of closing down the Bellchapel addiction clinic, which will spell disaster for Krystal's family.

She joins Colin's campaign and vows to help him keep Bellchapel open.

Terri is struggling to keep clean in spite of Bellchapel's help. When her grandmother Cath dies of a stroke – for which Parminder is unfairly blamed by many – she nearly relapses and is saved only by the fact that her dealer, Obbo, is out of town. When he returns she is persuaded by Krystal to not use again, but then fails to believe her daughter when Krystal is raped by Obbo. This leads Krystal to formulate a plan: by having her boyfriend Fats' baby, she will be able to get her own council house away from her mother and keep her younger brother Robbie.

Andrew, Sukhvinder and Gaia Bawden (Kay's daughter) get jobs at the Mollisons' café despite being the children of pro-Fielders. Andrew goes further in his own personal campaign against his father by hacking the parish council website and writing a post about his father's purchase of stolen goods and the cash-in-hand work that he does after hours at his job. Andrew posts this under the name of 'The _ Ghost _ of _ Barry _ Fairbrother'. His actions cause his father to withdraw his candidacy and take out his humiliation violently on his family. Andrew is still pleased with what he has achieved. He does, however, start to feel guilty later when his father loses his job.

Sukhvinder is the next disgruntled child to use 'The _ Ghost _ of _ Barry _ Fairbrother' to punish her parent – in this case her mother, Parminder. Sukhvinder self-harms as a result of her mother's disdainful treatment of her and Fats' relentless bullying. Sick of her mother's appalling treatment of her, Sukhvinder posts on the website that Parminder was in love with Barry Fairbrother. Fats is the next 'ghost' to humiliate a pro-Fielder. After overhearing his father say that he never wanted to adopt him, Fats decides to post about Colin's OCD and resulting tendency to falsely convince himself that he is a paedophile.

THE LEGACY OF BARRY FAIRBROTHER

In spite of the attacks by Barry's "ghost", the pro-Fielders continue to work towards their political goals. A meeting at Tessa Wall's house sees Kay brief Parminder on the statistics regarding the Bellchapel addiction centre, but Parminder finds her mind wandering. She wonders if she did have feelings for Barry, and concludes that, although she is vaguely of the political inclination that Bellchapel must remain open and the Fields a part of Pagford, her heart is not really in it. Colin is strongly in favour of Kay's pro-Bellchapel arguments in relation to Terri Weedon even though he rails against her daughter Krystal at school. Parminder is unable to argue coherently in favour of her position at the next parish council meeting, instead accusing Howard Mollison of hypocrisy (he complains about the cost to the NHS of drug users even though he costs the health service a fortune because he over-eats) and storming out in tears. She is suspended for breaching doctor-patient confidentiality.

On the day of the election the pro-Fielders go out to vote but their efforts are in vain, as Miles is elected. Samantha, who did not even vote for her husband, is forced to go to his election party, which is doubling as Howard's birthday party, despite her best efforts to be out of town. She drinks too much and ends up kissing Andrew Price. Miles' sister Pat, who is angry that her lesbian partner was not invited properly, shares Samantha's disdain for Howard and Shirley. Pat also reveals to Andrew that she once caught Howard cheating on Shirley with Maureen. Andrew, who feels slightly guilty for getting his father fired, posts this information on the council website, again under the name of 'The _ Ghost _ of _ Barry _ Fairbrother'.

The morning after the party, chaos ensues. Samantha admits to a furious Miles that she did not vote for him and is unsure if she still loves him. Shirley sees the allegations of adultery against her husband, and plans to stab him with Andrew Price's EpiPen. When she approaches him, however, she finds him having a heart attack. Gavin, having finally broken up with Kay, tells a mortified Mary that he is in love with her and is rebuffed. Krystal goes home to find that Obbo has stayed over and Terri has relapsed. She takes Robbie into Pagford and tries to get pregnant by Fats. Whilst the two are having sex, Robbie wanders off and falls in the river. Despite Sukhvinder jumping in to try and save him, Robbie dies. Krystal, in her despair, commits suicide by overdosing on her mother's heroin and in doing so achieves "her only ambition: she had joined her brother where nobody could part them" (p. 481).

In the aftermath of the Weedons' deaths, the people of Pagford reassess their lives, as people often do in the wake of a tragedy. Fats begins to question his behaviour and takes responsibility for all of the posts made by 'The _ Ghost _ of _ Barry _ Fairbrother' in an attempt to atone for his actions. Shirley attends to her recovering husband and takes her anger out on Maureen by overruling her ideas for the business in Howard's absence. Parminder steps down from the parish council and works on her relationship with Sukhvinder, who has stopped self-harming and organises Krystal and Robbie's joint funeral. Samantha reconciles with Miles and decides to stand for Parminder's vacant council seat and work to defend the Bellchapel clinic. Kay decides to move back to London with Gaia, and hangs up on Gavin when he pathetically tries to restart their relationship. Krystal is remembered fondly by her peers at her funeral while Terri is half-carried out of the church.

CHARACTER STUDY

BARRY FAIRBROTHER

Barry Fairbrother does not survive beyond the first few pages of the novel, and yet his presence is perhaps stronger than that of any other single character. He is a friendly, funny pillar of the community. Alongside his full time job, he is a councillor on the parish council, coaches the girls' rowing team and finds time besides to play squash with his friend Gavin and spend time with his wife and four children. He is a champion of the Fields, the nearby council estate where he grew up, and fights on the parish council for the Fields to remain a part of Pagford. He mentors Krystal Weedon, a fellow 'Fielder', and is resented by his wife for the time he devotes to Krystal and the Fields – time that she thinks could be better spent with his family. Barry's death is the catalyst of the events of the novel.

KRYSTAL WEEDON

Krystal Weedon is a teenager from the Fields who lives with her mother Terri, a drug addict who often prostitutes herself, and her younger brother Robbie. Krystal has never met her two older siblings as they were taken into care before she was born. Krystal is very troubled due to her chaotic home life: she is barely literate, lashes out violently and often truants, drinks and has underage/unprotected sex (including with her cousin). Despite all of this, Krystal is good at heart, as evidenced by her love for her younger brother Robbie, and the time she saved Andrew Price by alerting the teachers to the fact that he was having an allergic reaction.

Krystal begins to improve when Barry Fairbrother takes her on as his protégé, encouraging her to row and getting her an interview with the local newspaper. Things begin to go badly wrong for Krystal after Barry's death. Not only has her mentor gone, but the victory of anti-Fields councillors results in her mother relapsing and her world falling apart. Despite Krystal's best attempts to remove herself and her brother from their dangerous home life with Terri, her life ends in tragedy. Krystal's death provokes some self-reflection among some of the citizens of Pagford.

HOWARD MOLLISON

Howard Mollison is the owner of a local shop (which is expanding to include a café) and the leader of the parish council, or as he prefers to put it, 'first citizen' of Pagford. His politics are right-wing and he is virulently opposed to the Fields, which he thinks have tarnished Pagford. He also displays casual racism and often gropes the bottom of his daughter-in-law, Samantha. He is also in favour of the closure of the Bellchapel clinic, as he believes that impoverished people choose to be poor, conveniently forgetting the fact that he started his business with a large loan from his mother.

He is a very overweight, very unattractive man, but is adored by his wife Shirley and his business partner Maureen, with whom he has had at least one affair in the past. He loses the confidence of his wife when she finds out about his past indiscretions, but fails to experience her wrath as he suffers his second heart attack. He does not draw any comparison between the cost of drug abuse to the health service and the cost of his own heart surgeries which are a direct result of his choice to over-eat. He is hypocritical and perhaps the most unsympathetic character in the novel.

SAMANTHA MOLLISON

Samantha Mollison is defined throughout the novel by her frustration. Due to poor performance she is forced to close her shop selling outsized bras, and finds that her husband is largely uninterested. She is constantly criticised by her mother-in-law Shirley, who reminds her often that she and Howard are paying for Samantha's daughters' private education. She allows Howard to greet her by touching her bottom in order to get back at Shirley.

She is sexually frustrated in her marriage, which came about too soon due to her unplanned pregnancy with her first daughter Lexie. Samantha resents watching her husband turn into Howard day by day. She shows her feelings by drinking too much at social events and embarrassing her husband (and often herself). She fixates on a young boy band member (from a group her daughters follow) and thinks about him whenever her daily life is frustrating her. She even buys tickets for herself and her younger daughter Libby to see the band in London, but is eventually unable to go. After drunkenly kissing Andrew Price she realises that she finally needs to let go of her lost twenties and face up to her current problems.

PARMINDER JAWANDA

Parminder Jawanda is a Sikh GP who moved to Pagford from Birmingham. She had an arranged marriage to her husband, surgeon Vikram, and has three children: Jaswant, Rajpal and Sukhvinder. Her youngest child disappoints her, as she struggles with academic work due to her dyslexia, but Parminder often accuses her of being lazy. On a wall in the family home her elder two children make appearances in family photos almost twice as much as Sukhvinder does, which Tessa Wall notes as being incredibly cruel.

Parminder is on the pro-Fielder side of the parish council, and though her politics do generally align with the idea of collectivism and left-wing thought, she is not ultimately that interested in the fate of the Fields. Her interest in the council has more to do with Barry Fairbrother, who she considers to be a very close friend. She remembers how much she would laugh when she was around him and wonders if there is any truth in Sukhvinder's post about her being in love with Barry. She ultimately leaves the parish council and resolves to pay more attention to her family, and in particular her youngest daughter.

SUKHVINDER JAWANDA

Sukhvinder Jawanda is a teenager in the same class as Andrew Price and Fats Wall. The latter bullies her mercilessly, both in person and online. Her relationship with her mother is strained because Sukhvinder is less intelligent and less attractive than her two older siblings, Jaswant and Rajpal, which frustrates Parminder. Despite getting on well with the rest of her family, Sukhvinder is driven to self-harm, cutting herself on her arms in the dead of night. Things begin to look up for her when she is befriended by the pretty new student from London, Gaia.

Sukhvinder gets a job with Gaia at the Mollisons' café, which enrages Parminder. Sukhvinder takes revenge against her mother by posting on the parish council website that Parminder was in love with Barry Fairbrother. This conveys her struggle with face-to-face confrontation. She develops throughout the course of the novel and shows herself to be brave and caring. She jumps in the river in an attempt to save Robbie. Although unsuccessful, she emerges from the river a hero, and finds the confidence to stop harming herself and takes charge of organising Krystal and Robbie's joint funeral.

ANDREW PRICE

Andrew Price is a teenager with an unhappy home life due to his father's abusive nature. Simon Price lashes out at his family members frequently and without reason. He also has cruel nicknames for his sons: he calls Andrew 'pizza-face' on account of his acne, and calls his other son Paul 'Pauline'. Andrew despises his father and also has a low opinion of his mother for tolerating her husband's behaviour. Andrew spends most of the novel obsessed with Gaia Bawden, and takes a job at the Mollisons' café just so that he can spend time with her. His best friend is Fats Wall, whose bullying of Sukhvinder he tolerates, though it makes him feel uneasy.

FATS WALL

Stuart 'Fats' Wall is Tessa and Colin's adopted son. He spends his time looking for ways to anger his parents and obsesses over the notion of authenticity. He finds his parents to be completely inauthentic and feels that this justifies his contempt for them. He seeks out Krystal Weedon for sex even though he does not have feelings for her – he feels that responding to his instinct for sex is the most authentic thing he can do. Like his peers Andrew and Sukhvinder, he takes revenge on his parents by hacking the parish council website and sharing their darkest secrets with the community. Fats, along with perhaps Howard Mollison, is one of the cruellest characters in the novel, as evidenced by his bullying of Sukhvinder Jawanda and callous using of Krystal Weedon.

KAY BAWDEN

Kay is a social worker who moves to Pagford from London to be with her partner, Gavin Hughes. She does this in order to try and create a normal family life with a stable father figure for her daughter Gaia, but fails to see that Gavin is not as invested in the relationship as she is. She is very caring, and goes out of her way to help the Weedons when she is working as their social worker. She is frustrated that she is not able to continue after her predecessor comes back from leave. She works with Colin to try and get a pro-Fielder elected to the parish council, and even goes to Krystal's house after hearing of Robbie's death. Ultimately, she finds the strength to definitively end her relationship with Gavin (even after he tries to once again make up with her) and moves back to London with Gaia, thus fixing her difficult relationship with her daughter.

ANALYSIS

RESPONSIBILITY

'Responsibility' was actually the working title of *The Casual Vacancy* before Rowling found the technical term for Barry Fairbrother's vacant council seat, and it is clear to see why. The theme of responsibility is ever-present throughout the novel, and questions are raised about social responsibility and also the extent to which responsibility should lie with the individual. The treatment of this theme also touches on the nature vs. nurture debate, particularly relating to the younger characters: are they responsible for their actions or should the blame lie with the parents who raised them badly?

The two political groups in the novel fall on either side of the social responsibility debate. Barry and the pro-Fielders believe in collectivism and the idea that the state should bear responsibility for its less fortunate citizens. Howard and the anti-Fielders, on the other hand, believe in individual responsibility, and ultimately believe that the poor choose to be poor because of an innate weakness.

"There was nothing, as far as Howard could see, to stop the Fielders [...] pulling themselves together as a community [...] and taking jobs; nothing at all. So Howard was forced to draw the conclusion that they were choosing, of their own free will, to live the way they lived, and that the estate's air of slightly threatening degradation was nothing more than a physical manifestation of ignorance and indolence." (p. 61)

Rowling clearly disagrees with Howard's hypothesis, and argues against it by presenting the desperate case of Terri Weedon. Terri was sexually abused as a child by her father, with whom she lived after her mother walked out. One day Terri's father threw a pan of chip fat at her, burning her badly. She temporarily lived with her grandmother for a few days after this before her father came to bring her home. This is presented as a turning point in Terri's life: had she been permitted to live with her grandmother Cath, then her life, and by extension her children's lives, might have turned out very differently. Not only did Howard not, as far as the reader can tell, suffer childhood abuse, he also started his successful business with a sizeable loan from his mother, the likes of which Terri could only dream. Howard's suggestion that Terri chose her poverty, rather than being reduced to it by these numerous setbacks and abuses, is presented as risible.

RELIGIOUS IMAGERY

There is a strong religious theme to much of the novel's imagery. The most obvious example of this is Barry's lingering presence in Pagford even after his fatal aneurysm, and the implication that there can be life after death. Samantha Mollison even says that she thought she saw Barry even though she knew he had already died at this point. This is explained away as her probably seeing one of his brothers, but the suggestion of the ghostly is clear. Because the novel begins and ends with death, the local church features twice as a setting, and provokes feelings both of spirituality and of discomfort in various different characters. Krystal is even said to join Robbie "where nobody could part them" (p. 481) when she overdoses: this phrasing is strongly suggestive of an afterlife.

The ghostly is, of course, most heavily implicit in the user name Andrew, Sukhvinder and Fats use to post messages about their parents on the council website: The _ Ghost _ of _ Barry _ Fairbrother. The use of the word 'ghost' is not only religious because the existence of ghosts points to religious teachings on the afterlife and the human soul, but also because The _ Ghost _ of _ Barry _ Fairbrother reveals secrets that the victims believed no one else knew. The ghost therefore has connotations of an omniscient being who is secretly observing Colin's OCD, Parminder's feelings for Barry (feelings that she was not even aware of herself), Simon's stolen computer and Howard's adultery. But it is not God witnessing these foibles, but rather one of each individual's children.

Another example of religious imagery in the novel comes not from Christianity, but from Sikhism. In one of the earlier parts of the novel, Parminder muses over her attempts to teach her children about their religion. She thinks about the story of Guru Nanak submerging himself in a river for three days, and emerging having spoken to God and been enlightened. This imagery is clearly linked to Sukhvinder's time underwater as she attempts to save Robbie from drowning in the river. When she comes up, although she was too late to save Robbie, she has changed. She no longer feels the need to self-harm, and is more confident than ever, as evidenced by the determination with which she fundraises and organises a joint funeral for Krystal and Robbie. She has, much liked Guru Nanak, been enlightened.

MULTIPLE PERSPECTIVES

The novel is told from the perspective of a multitude of different characters, although it is always written in the third person. This allows Rowling to present arguments from characters with differing views without necessarily having to engineer scenes in which these characters debate each other (although there are some such scenes in the novel). Rowling often writes characters' thoughts as they reflect on the issues facing the community. The limitations of each character's perspective are also highlighted. For example, Howard and the anti-Fielders claim that they cannot see what is stopping the Fielders from sorting out their lives. But the very things that prevent Terri and Krystal Weedon from living normal, happy lives (such as childhood trauma and sexual abuse) are the things that Howard cannot see because he segregates himself from the Fields and is unwilling to acknowledge that poverty is not a choice.

The use of multiple perspectives also gives the reader the ability to judge events in context. The reader learns early on in the novel that when Krystal Weedon was a child, she punched Lexie Mollison in the face so hard that she knocked out two of her teeth. We learn this in a section of the novel that is written from Howard's perspective, and so we learn nothing of the context. In a later part of the novel written from Krystal's perspective, we learn that in primary school Lexie Mollison handed everyone in their class a birthday party invitation except Krystal, whom she walked past "with – as Krystal remembered it – her nose in the air" (p. 247). This is obviously not an excuse for violence, but it does contextualise Krystal's behaviour. From Howard's retelling of the incident, one might think that Krystal had lashed out for no reason and was inherently violent.

While the reader's impression of Krystal improves when we hear from different, more sympathetic perspectives about her behaviour, other characters are diminished in the reader's eyes when they are examined from a different viewpoint. Parminder is a good example of this: while she comes across as somewhat cold, she is sympathetic to the pro-Fielders' arguments and feels compassion for those less fortunate than her. When the novel's perspective switches to Sukhvinder, however, the reader learns that Parminder treats her youngest child differently because she is not as pretty and clever as her older siblings. She does not listen to her daughter and fails to take into account that her academic difficulties are not all down to laziness; she does suffer from dyslexia. In the same way that the reader is slowly drawn toward the conclusion that characters like Krystal are not all bad, it is slowly revealed that some of the characters who are initially implied to be good are actually very flawed people, and even have the capacity to be cruel.

FURTHER REFLECTION

SOME QUESTIONS TO THINK ABOUT...

- Do you think the novel presents a positive or negative portrayal of village society? Explain your answer.
- Discuss the motivations of the people behind The _ Ghost _ of _ Barry _ Fairbrother.
- The novel tackles many issues relating to social breakdown: drug abuse, rape, prostitution. Where does Rowling place the responsibility for these social ills?
- Discuss the pros and cons of the use of multiple perspectives.
- Compare the novel with its television adaptation. How have the producers dealt with compressing such a long novel into three hour-long episodes? How successful are they?
- In your opinion, should the Fields remain a part of Pagford? Justify your answer.
- Discuss the generational gap in Pagford.
- Is Parminder right to label Howard a hypocrite? Why/why not?

We want to hear from you!
Leave a comment on your online library
and share your favourite books on social media!

FURTHER READING

REFERENCE EDITION

- Rowling, J.K. (2012) The Casual Vacancy. London: Little, Brown.

ADAPTATIONS

- *The Casual Vacancy*. (2015) [TV series]. Jonny Campbell. Dir. UK: Brontë Film and Television.

MORE FROM BRIGHTSUMMARIES.COM

- Reading guide – *Harry Potter and the Philosopher's Stone* by J.K. Rowling.

- Reading guide – *Harry Potter and the Chamber of Secrets* by J.K. Rowling.

- Reading guide – *Harry Potter and the Prisoner of Azkaban* by J.K. Rowling.

- Reading guide – *Harry Potter and the Goblet of Fire* by J.K. Rowling.

- Reading guide – *Harry Potter and the Order of the Phoenix* by J.K. Rowling.

- Reading guide – *Harry Potter and the Half-Blood Prince* by J.K. Rowling.

- Reading guide – *Harry Potter and the Deathly Hallows* by J.K. Rowling.

Although the editor makes every effort to
verify the accuracy of the information published,
BrightSummaries.com accepts no responsibility for
the content of this book.

www.brightsummaries.com

Ebook EAN: 9782808017343

Paperback EAN: 9782808017350

Legal Deposit: D/2019/12603/34

Cover: © Primento

Digital conception by Primento, the digital partner of
publishers.